[RE]BIRTH

[RE]BIRTH

Self-Transformation over Tea and Tarot

MARY-CLAIRE HANLON
Australia

Copyright © 2019 by Mary-Claire Hanlon.

ISBN-9781645506607

All rights reserved. No part of this book may be reproduced or transmitted in any form or by any means, electronic or mechanical, including photocopying, recording, or by any information storage and retrieval system, without permission in writing from the author.

The views expressed in this work are solely those of the author and do not necessarily reflect the views of the publisher, and the publisher hereby disclaims any responsibility for them.

Matchstick Literary
1-888-306-8885
orders@matchliterary.com

Dedication

To my parents, who showed me a good way to live, and gave me the means to achieve it.

Contents

Part 1: The Major Arcana 1
  Chapter 1: I recognise my Self 3
    In the beginning was the fool. 3
    When the fool awoke, he found himself before a very
    great man. 4
    And then he saw a woman. She was beautiful and dark. 6
    He felt full: full of something about to happen,
    though he didn't know what. 8
    The lovely voluptuous woman had met her match in
    this great man. 9
    The bark seemed to transform into a wizened old man
    in a cloak, with a long beard and a staff. 10
  Chapter 2: I recognise You 12
    His heart swelled with passion. 12
    He brought everything he had. 13
    Ultimately, the lion and the unicorn beat the fool. He
    was spent. He gave up. 13
    The fool started to change his mind about being with
    his Lover. 14
    He studied the cycles of life; and grew in wisdom. 16
    Patience without Prejudice. 16
    Justice decided to get another perspective. 17
  Chapter 3: A new perspective 20
    Suddenly, he saw that the seeds he planted had
    sprouted and grown. 20
    He dreamed of a woman making the impossible with
    the improbable. 21

It seemed he was rooted to the spot; shackled as it were, to the sight of her..22

Chapter 4: Shock **24**
Suddenly the world shook...24
The night was dark, until Venus and Jupiter appeared in the sky...25
The Lover had to go on, without knowing where she was, who she was, or what to do next. 25
So, what was hidden, was revealed. 27
A prophet changes the world..28

Part 2: The Minor Arcana **31**
Chapter 5: Kings and Queens..................................... **37**
Chapter 6: The little children of the Minor Arcana **41**
Show me the baby!!..41
Terrible Twos (not really, not terrible at all)................43
Three is a crowd 44
Awesome Foursome versus the Gang of Four...............46
Flying Fives 47
Sweet, Serene Sixes!...50
Sticky Sevens 51
Mates with Eights 54
Nearly There, Nines 56
Tens are too much of a good thing! 57
Chapter 7: The teenagers of the Minor Arcana................ **60**
Prince and Princess / Page and Knight........................60

Part 3: Bringing it all together **63**
Transform your relationships 63
Transform your learning and teaching........................65
Transform your work and vocation 65
Transform your community 65
Transform the world!..66

Acknowledgments

I would like to thank the many people who have helped me along the way – those who listened without prejudice or judgement, who led me toward my various destinies, who waited patiently for me to arrive at my many destinations along the way.. I am thankful for the selfless few who took the time to read this manuscript, listen to me read it aloud, and who discussed the concepts with me, so I could tell if it made sense (especially to someone unfamiliar with the tarot).

Those angels know who they are, and they have their place in Heaven.

This has been an adventure into self-discovery, and a joyful uncovering of what has been hidden or even repressed. I am a human, not without fault, but also a shining example of what is possible with love and support.

With gratitude, Mary-Claire.

"I acknowledge the traditional custodians of Australia and
their continuing connection to land, sea and community.

I respect the elders past and present and express
my heartfelt apology for the injustices endured
by Aboriginal people of our nation.

I will continue to strive, day by day, for my thoughts
and actions to reflect these truths and sentiments."

Introduction

Firstly, I want you to get comfortable! Grab a "cuppa" (as we say in Australia), put your feet up, and relax. This is going to be fun! Your new book (this one) is divided into parts and can be read in different stages. Each stage can be read at any time, but you might prefer to start at the beginning and just go with the flow to the end of the book, and then enjoy the random-opening-read once you understand how it works. Although, having said that, you might also find that in opening this book at a random place, you will find the answer you seek right now. Follow your heart.

As you read, you might like to doodle the pictures that you imagine. You might like to draw what you imagine into a separate book (like an unlined journal) or on cards, or you might even enjoy painting it! As you read, draw about the vision that **you** have. For example, if you read about a person with a little dog as a companion, draw this as you imagine it. Colour your picture and embellish as you see fit. The more intricate that you make your picture, the more articulate – that is, the more you add, the more your Inner Self will speak to you, and you will learn about your Self. You could even go on to embroider your images or craft something out of timber, clay or other materials so that the more you use your hands, the more you connect your imagination to your reality.

This book, your book, uses tarot as a tool for reflection, meditation, and self-transformation (not divination). Don't be put off by my reference to the tarot – I won't be using it to read your fortune, I'll be using it purely as a tool for inspiration. Tarot cards are divided into the Major Arcana and the Minor Arcana (arcana is a term often used to describe something secret or mysterious, but I use it as "library" or "collection"). They are basically two decks of cards that ended up together. Plenty of other books will tell you the history, but that's not relevant to this book. Just imagine an art gallery curator collected certain works of art because they were important generally (for example, the Minor Arcana), and because they followed a theme (for example, the Major Arcana). Everyone who sees those works of art will appreciate them differently.

This first part of your book is an allegory (a story that sets the scene), using the Major Arcana, to help you know where you are in life. You will be invited to draw the pictures described for yourself, so you can recognise your Self in the story. The second part of the book tells another part of the story – how the Minor Arcana of the tarot represents the challenges of life that impact on how we see ourselves and the situations in which we find ourselves, and the people around us at the time.

The third part of the book brings it all together. Imagine learning who you could have been, who you are, and also, who you could become! We combine the earlier knowledge into life skills. Finally, you might like to try meditative practice using this book as inspiration. This can be as easy as using one image to think about and ponder, or having a go at story-telling. Go with the flow. Follow your heart.

I want to make a few things clear, before going any further.

Firstly, what is presented here is not entirely new. I am thankful for wisdom passed on to me by tarot writers more knowledgeable than me, and in particular through Thirteen's "Tarot Card Meanings" and "The Instant Tarot Reader" by Monty Farber and Amy Zerner. Their inspiration led me to write this book because I could see the potential of the tarot to resonate with a person's experience, and for that I am deeply thankful. I read those books (and many others) while an undergraduate at The University of Newcastle obtaining my Bachelor of Science, as well as my postgraduate studies (I have Honours in Psychology and a PhD in Psychiatry). So, my reading and practice have always answered a search for balance, of science and faith, of courage and love.

Secondly, I have not written this book so that you can learn how to tell a fortune (your own or for someone else). There are already many books on that topic and I don't see a need to add to that library. Instead, I wrote this book simply to help myself and others grow through understanding our psychological makeup and interpersonal tensions. Think of this book as a part of your own "Transformation Retreat".

Finally, yes, I am a catholic, and so my own faith will probably colour what is written here; and that faith is that *~if God exists, then nothing is impossible*. My aim will always be your self-transformation, on your own terms, and my advice will always be – "Go with the flow. Follow your heart."

Part 1:
The Major Arcana

The two decks of the tarot are called the Major Arcana and the Minor Arcana. Arcana sometimes means "mysteries" or "secrets", but for me, it means "library" or "collection". The Minor Arcana is simply like the deck of cards with which many of us have grown up–playing games of chance. The Major Arcana is something different; and I like to think of it as "the fool's journey". We all resonate with the fool. We are occasionally too trusting for our own good; other times we don't trust enough. Sometimes, our ideas are genius, while at others, just plain stupid. We all experience embarrassment, and we can all enjoy grandeur. You get the picture. We are who we see ourselves to be, nothing more or less.

The fool's journey follows a series of cards that usually have specific names and numbers, but we are not concerned with those aspects in this book. We are concerned with how to use the Major Arcana as a tool for reflection, meditation, self-discovery and self-transformation. So, I invite you to come on the fool's journey ....

Chapter 1:
I recognise my Self

In the beginning was the fool.

The fool trusted himself and had faith in a benevolent Universe that was kind and caring. The fool was one with the Universe and content with life. The fool seemed to have been born with a companion; a little white puppy, a faithful friend who was always there. The fool had no home, but didn't seem to need one. He had a pack on a stick, a whistle on his lips, and a song in his heart. He skipped through meadows in merry attire, oblivious to the blue skies above and the landscape below.

It seemed as if the fool had always been. He had no memory of an earlier life. He just Was. He and his little dog came skipping to the end of the meadow, one sunny blue-skied day, and having had no memory of anything befalling him before this day, the fool skipped towards the edge. His little dog chewed at his ankle to get his attention – to possibly warn him, but the fool had no knowledge of the outcome of stepping off the edge.

He stepped off.

Blissfully, excitedly, he discovered that he was flying through the air. He began hurtling towards the earth below and it felt funny, so he laughed with merry abandon and little convulsions that came from deep within his belly. He didn't feel that this was scary, but different to the feeling of skipping and flying!

Something caught him on the lace of his shoe. His body jerked, and then he swung; mid-air, and looked up to see what had stopped his descent. A twig on the end of a branch had caught him. So, he dangled there, accepting the situation for what it was. Upside-down.

He saw the world from a different perspective. He could see up the cliff, and the birds nesting in cracks in the rock. He wouldn't have noticed them if this hadn't happened. He wouldn't have made this happy discovery! He looked down and could see a vast plain with a river and white-water, with towns and valleys .. From this vantage point, he could see people as small as ants. So much detail, in such a big picture. He laughed again at the sight!

It was fascinating! He dangled there, suspended, for some time. He had no concept of time, and no need to be anywhere, and so he was content to stay there. Time passed.

He began noticing that the blood was rushing to his head and he didn't feel so good. So, he began wriggling to try to free himself. It didn't work. He was trapped! All alone, his little dog at the top of the cliff sat, while the fool dangled helplessly below.

The fool had no idea how to get help, because he had no memory of this type of thing happening previously (he had no memory of anything, including people). So, he waited. And waited. And he waited still. He passed out.

When the fool awoke, he found himself before a very great man.

This man exuded magic. The fool wasn't sure if the man was real, if he was dreaming, or if the Magician was actually himself in a mirror. Hard to tell. He was magnetic; his words electric.

The Magician stood behind a table, and on the table lay the fool's stick and pack. The pack-cloth was unfurled, exposing its contents. There was a knife, a cup and a seed on the table, along with the stick

[RE]BIRTH

and the cloth. These items seemed to be heavy with significance for the Magician. Without words, he showed the fool that he had all he needed to survive, and that what he needed up that cliff, was the knife to cut himself loose so he could drop to the earth below and keep moving forward. The knife's not a weapon, but a tool.

The fool could tell the Magician was an awesome man —his vibe was phenomenal! But he didn't really "get" the depth of what the Magician wanted to tell him.

Groggily, the fool walked away, his little dog catching up to him. Little did the fool know that it was his dog's barking that caught the attention of the Magician so he could be cut free.

The fool walked on, his dog pattering beside him, and he began to skip again. Again, he skipped right off the cliff! Again, he hurtled over and was caught on the branch. The twig had broken, but the branch was still there. The fool dangled. The fool began to think. He thought of the Magician, and wondered if there were any other interesting (and possibly just as odd) people out there? He became keen to discover them! He felt a sense of urgency to find them and meet them. He wriggled to try to free himself, to no avail. He was trapped, again. But this time, he was frustrated. He didn't dangle there thinking about the pretty view. This time, he felt impatient. Even, angry. Though, he wasn't angry with himself, or the dog, or the Magician. He was just angry that something unexpectedly wonderful happened recently (he met someone amazing) and he wanted to discover more but couldn't. He was impatient!

He wriggled, and wriggled, until – exhausted – he gave up. He felt the frustration. He felt the trappedness. The isolation. The fear. The hopelessness and helplessness. Forlorn in his feelings, he wept.

Just as he resigned himself to being trapped here forever, the emotions subsided and the boredom engulfing him, somehow the grip on his leg loosened and he fell.

He was back at the river, this time in the river; the white water gushing past rocks and boulders, causing hazardous rips and eddies in the dark recesses. It bashed him against hidden dangers lurking below. His bruised and battered body felt --- terrible!

The fool was suddenly aware of hunger, and thirst, as well as this horrible battered and bruised feeling. He was pummelled and paralysed with pain. A log came hurtling toward him and, luckily, he grabbed hold of it, launching himself onto it. Finally, he was able to breathe, though not able to direct where the log would take him. It bumped into rocks; it snagged on branches. He was still trapped, just differently!

AND THEN HE SAW A WOMAN. SHE WAS BEAUTIFUL AND DARK.

Not classically pretty, but intriguing. Enticing. Mysterious. Behind a veiled pavilion. The moonlight seemed to shimmer on her glorious dark, smooth skin. It seemed as if she called to him, or rather, called to the log and it responded by floating effortlessly toward her. The fool came to the water's edge where she stood, and she offered him a hand to stand on dry land. He sighed deeply as he took it.

Overwhelmed with relief, he sobbed onto her chest. It wasn't an "ample bosom" by any means, but what would he know? She was the first woman he'd ever seen, and she was like an angel. Calm. Serene. Elegant. Refined. Strong but soft.

She sat down in front of her pavilion before him and allowed him to rest. He forgot his hunger, his thirst, his aches and pains. He became aware of only – Being. And for some reason, the Magician came to mind, and he thought "A-ha!" The fool realised what the Magician tried to tell him. "You already have everything you need". It was as if this knowledge was under lock and key, and this woman, who seemed to know and feel everything, unlocked the Magician's secret. Without her, the fool might never have understood.

You have everything you need.

[RE]BIRTH

While the Magician's power was like air, like thunder and lightning, like wind and storm, the High Priestess's power was like water – purifying, cleansing, nourishing, nurturing. Fresh.

The fool finally felt restored, and he thanked the High Priestess and went on his way. He walked now, noticing where his steps fell, choosing to step respectfully on earth that was secure, looking ahead to see where he could (and should not) go. His little dog, ever faithful friend, came along. He walked by the river awhile, and came upon a boat. He decided that because he survived the white water and the dark rips and eddies, he would like to try the water again, in the boat. He stepped in, followed by his dog, and sat in the boat. His weight was enough to launch it, and off he floated, down the river. At times, he sat, looking out to the villages and forests, and at other times, he lay back, looking up into the night sky, marvelling at the stars and moon, the shining planets – not knowing what they were or how far away. He was so moved, that he wept in wonder. And, taking the cloth and untying it from his stick, he wept into the cloth, using it as a (rather large) handkerchief.

There was no paddle; there were no oars. He hadn't looked for them because he didn't know they were needed, like a rudder, or an anchor. Sometimes, the boat stayed very still. At other times, he drifted, while at other times the boat raced through the gushing waters. He wasn't sure what to do, and so he just went with the flow. He trusted that it would take him somewhere safe. He hoped it would take him to meet someone interesting, like the Magician and the High Priestess. He looked forward to the adventures to which it would bring him.

At one point, his little craft was caught on something in the water. And so he took his stick and used it to shove his boat away from the entrapment. Another time, after he had rinsed his cloth clean, he noticed the wind whipping it up. He tied two corners to his stick, a third to a side of the boat, and held the fourth, and discovered (by making a sail) he could travel faster than before. Ah yes, he thought, I have everything I need!

HE FELT FULL: FULL OF SOMETHING ABOUT TO HAPPEN, THOUGH HE DIDN'T KNOW WHAT.

Not a bloated feeling, but a pregnant feeling. Expectant. Radiant. Glowing. He felt the need to put down roots. To find a place to sit quietly and listen to the birds and frogs. To make something from the earth and water with his hands. His boat led him there. It washed ashore and out he stepped, onto dry land. He felt moved to plant his seed at this place; and as he dug a hole that filled with water from the river, he felt grateful for the people who had entered his life and were to come. He sat in the sunshine and peace; and absorbed all the goodness of life.

After a while, he got up, and he and his little dog went for a walk. He came to a building of vast proportions, made of clay and earth and straw, with a sturdy roof and windows which let in the light but not harsh winds. It was a home and a castle. He entered through a gateway and encountered a voluptuous woman. She was lovely. So lovely, he wanted to hug her, and he did. Maternally, she responded, with the warmest embrace. She gave him milk and cookies, and later, food and wine, and listened to his stories. She showed him to a room, where he could bathe and sleep, and told him that he could tell her anything. She would listen, and she would not judge. He felt safe with her. She was regal, yet earthy. Feminine, yet sturdy. Soft but strong. Her bosoms were ample!! When the fool looked at her, he imagined hundreds of little children coming to her and calling her "Mamma!" In her eyes, he saw the joy of future generations, and the love of family.

For the first time in his life, he felt home. He felt protected and nurtured and cared for. He brushed his teeth, bathed and changed into soft pyjamas, and lay down on the softest biggest bed. His pillow cradled his weary head, he closed his sleepy eyes, and he fell fast asleep.

In the morning, the fool put on clean clothes and combed his hair, and went looking for the lovely voluptuous woman. When he found her, she was sitting – rather regally – on an impressive throne, next to an equally impressive man.

THE LOVELY VOLUPTUOUS WOMAN HAD MET HER MATCH IN THIS GREAT MAN.

He was sensible, wise and fair. The fool approached, grateful for the hospitality he received from the Empress and curious about the Emperor.

The Emperor bid him come closer, and the fool did so. The Emperor could see that the fool was at the start of his journey, and gave him sage advice. The Emperor told the fool to make sure he had a place to call home, even if it was just in his heart; to plant seeds and nurture them so he would always have something for the future; to learn something new every day to keep life exciting; and to have faith in himself, so he could confidently make his dreams come true. All else would follow, so not to worry. And then the Emperor held out his hands and placed into the fool's palms 20 seeds, to plant whenever he learned a lesson, and sent the fool on his way.

The fool thanked the Emperor for his wise advice and as he left the kingdom, he planted the first two seeds – one for the Empress, because she taught him kindness and hospitality, and one for the Emperor, because his lesson was to plan for the future. He planted those seeds with the first near a little dam; and hoped that they would grow into good strong trees to which he would return again in the future.

The little dam fed into a river and as he followed it, he found himself climbing a mountain. He followed the rocks uphill as the evening grew dark. It was hard to see. He couldn't even see his little dog trotting beside his ankles, but knew – somehow – that he was not alone.

After a while, he sat, and his eyes adjusted to the night's darkness. He saw the outline of leaves on trees and the roughness of their bark. And then something strange occurred.

The bark seemed to transform into a wizened old man in a cloak, with a long beard and a staff.

Dangling from his staff, was an old-fashioned lamp. The old man looked at the fool and started walking towards a cave, as if to say, 'follow me'. The fool and the dog followed him into the cave, and there the old man told him his tale. "Once upon a time", he said "I was passionate about a cause. I wanted to work for the glory of God."

The fool had no idea what the old man was talking about; and asked what he meant. The old man said that he believed there was a being greater than all of us, who made us and loves us. This being, God, is spirit, and has shared spirit with all of us. When we live, Spirit lives in us and through us as our soul. When we die, Spirit re-joins Spirit. Simple.

"But why?" the fool asked, and the old man's answer shocked him: "What does your heart say?" But the fool had no answer, so he listened to the old man, the Hierophant, all night. They talked about having a cause, a reason to be, a community. The fool became aware of believing.

The fool said that he loved all that he was learning and experiencing, but wanted to build something with his newfound knowledge. What if it all amounts to nothing? The Hierophant said that fear is a trap. Either you face your fear and in so doing, overcome it, or you let your fear hold you back. If you allow fear to stop you from moving forward then you open your life to injustice, greed, sorrow, and regret. If you face your fear, sure you might lose all you build, but you will still keep the experience and knowledge you had up to that point, and more – you will have new experience and knowledge, you will have hindsight and wisdom. You learn from your experiences, and sometimes they include your mistakes. It won't always be easy, and there are some fixes that won't be quick, but you will have everything you need. Just make it simple; be down-to-earth.

They talked about justice and injustice, about how humans can hurt others out of fear, but can also help each other out of compassion and love. "What is the greater path?" the Hierophant would say, and the fool's response would always be "to help". Simple. But at times, this too will take courage.

When the sky began to pale in the morning light, the Hierophant began to fade, but before he did he asked, "Do you believe?", to which the fool responded "yes"; "then bring heaven to earth". And with those last words, he disappeared, and the sun rose.

Bring the divine down-to-earth. Heaven-on-earth. God-with-us. Spirit-with-spirit. The fool felt that he learned a lesson here, and so he planted a fourth seed on the top of the mountain. And this time, he gave thanks for the people he had met on his journey, for the faithful friend who accompanied him, and for the adventures he was having in this strange world. He sent each one blessings, as he looked out from the peak, surveying the vast vista all around him. He patted his little dog, and cupped its sweet face in his hands. What a sweet little dog!

The fool decided that he wanted a cause, and that his cause would be to encourage all people to be kind to one another, like all his mentors had been to him. He felt passionate about it, and descending the mountain, he plotted how it could be achieved. He was quite certain about one thing: as much as he loved meeting all these interesting people (and spirits?), he was alone, and his mission was a solo mission. He would not be deterred.

CHAPTER 2:
I RECOGNISE YOU

HIS HEART SWELLED WITH PASSION.

He became aware of wanting. He wanted to make a difference to others, the way that others had made him different. And then, there she was. She was naked, alone and beautiful. She was The One. He was suddenly wanting her: passionately, physically, sexually. Uncontrollably.

He took her in his arms and devoured the scent of her hair and the touch of her skin. Passionately he made love to her, without realising what he was doing, and the effect it might have. She too wanted him and responded with equal passion.

Spent, they lay together on soft green grass under the midday sun. Their bodies warm in the sun's rays, and cooled by a gentle breeze against the glisten of post-coital sweat on their skin. He became suddenly aware that she was not in his plan, but he could not live without her. He sat up and looked straight into her eyes. He told her his plans and how they did not include her. She wept in her sorrow. Had she known, would she have given herself so freely, so wantonly? She would still have committed herself to him. He was The one.

And yet, she was not part of his plan. And to be honest, he had not been part of hers. Her cause was innocence. She had her life mapped out and had committed to virginity and chastity, and found herself having to make the same choice. They were happy alone, but now, passionate souls who were meant for each other.

She questioned his cause and his reasoning, and asked that if God were such a loving being, why would God expect him to be alone? Why would God bring them together only for them to be torn apart?

The fool and his Lover spoke at length, debated and even argued passionately about the choice to be made. Finally, the fool and his Lover decided, that instead of choosing between their cause and their Lover, they would combine them. This would mean a merge of alchemic proportions. The fool and his Lover brought their possessions together to live in each other's Universe.

He brought everything he had.

He brought his boat, his seeds, cup, knife, cloth and staff, and his little dog of course. She brought her wheels, a lion and a unicorn, a mirror and ropes. Hmm. How to bring these things together? How to make something of them? His Lover's lion and unicorn had been free, and now the fool, trying to impress his Lover, tethered them together with the ropes. He fixed her wheels to his boat, using his stick as an axel, and bid her join him in his new Chariot. He was feeling confident!

The lion and the unicorn tried to race in different directions. The Chariot sped over rocks and toppled over, coming apart. The fool got up, and tried again, determined to make this work. Because he had never come across a lion or a unicorn, he didn't know how dangerous each could be. He was confident that he could control them by uniting them. He tried again, and again, each time failing miserably and getting more and more frustrated. He was determined to succeed, no matter the cost, and so he kept trying.

Ultimately, the lion and the unicorn beat the fool. He was spent. He gave up.

The Lover got up and untied the lion and the unicorn, realising they weren't accustomed to being treated in this fashion. They were wild animals, with no desire to be whipped into line by an arrogant man.

The Lover tended to their wounds, bathing them using the fool's cloth soaked in water she collected in the fool's cup from the nearby river. She spoke softly to them, stroking them gently and lovingly. She told them that the fool didn't know what majestic creatures they both were, but that it was his cup and cloth that she used to tend to them so lovingly.

The lion and the unicorn, bowed their heads and allowed the Lover to tether them together. While tethered, she showed them their own reflection in the mirror, so that instead of seeing the other by their side, they saw self. They saw a kindred spirit instead of a foe. She walked them together under a tree, to escape the heat of the sun's rays. She led them together to the river to drink. All the while, she spoke softly to them both, telling them what wondrous and magnificent animals they were. Loving them equally; and making them happy.

Love gave her inner strength and courage. Love gave her kindness. Love gave her faith and hope and gentleness. And all of these, the Lover shared with her unicorn and lion.

They rested together overnight, and in the morning, the Lover achieved ~ with love ~ what the fool could not (with force). Gently, she tethered the lion and the unicorn together; and tied them to the boat-chariot. Off they went on their quest.

The fool started to change his mind about being with his Lover.

He was so sure that he could force his Lover's lion and unicorn together, and so startled that he couldn't, that the fool began to re-evaluate who he was. He thought about his solo quest, about his relationship to his Lover, and the influence of these strange animals. He loved his little dog, but he just didn't understand the unicorn and

[RE]BIRTH

the lion, nor did he understand the relationship his Lover had with them.

The fool began to think deeply about his relationship. He began to realise that he needed to reconnect with his inner self, and, as politely and gently as he could, he told his Lover that he would return to the mountaintop to talk with the Hierophant. His Lover, understanding that her fool needed to be alone to think, to pray, and to meditate, kissed his lips and held him tenderly one last time. They found a stream surrounded by willow trees and daffodils; and planted a fifth seed there together beside the boat. They expressed their gratitude in finding each other and in sharing love.

They parted, the best of friends, and resumed their solo quests. The fool took his little dog and his pack on a stick, and walked toward the mountain, looking for signs of the Hierophant.

Nowhere did the fool find his mentor. Instead, he wandered alone for days, sleeping in caves and under trees. Days turned to weeks, and weeks turned to months. The fool started growing hair where it had never been; and experiencing feelings he'd not encountered previously. He missed his Lover; and longed for a time that he could meet with her again. He thought of the Empress and the Emperor, and the lessons of hospitality and planning for the future. He thought of the High Priestess and the Magician, and how they pulled the veil from his eyes, so he could see that he had everything he needed. Sometimes he was thirsty and hungry, but other times food and fresh water were so plentiful that he could not help but be satisfied.

His beard grew, as he lived the life of a Hermit. One day, while walking through a forest, he came upon a lamp like the old Hierophant's. He was overjoyed! He found a way to make fire and lit the wick, and he meditated on all he had experienced. He was at peace.

He studied the cycles of life; and grew in wisdom.

He noticed that sometimes in his life, he had just been "lucky". Other times, he needed to listen, to pay attention, to try harder, and to let others guide him.

Nature showed him the cycles of life, and he learned the consequences of changing the direction of water, of moving earth, and of the winds across the skies. He watched animals as they interacted and saw that some would eventually produce an egg which could lead to a small and defenceless offspring, while others produced live baby versions of themselves. He wondered if that could have happened with him and his Lover. He paid closer attention to the timing of rutting and birth; and tried to calculate if it might have actually happened. Maybe, he had left his lover with child!

Suddenly, he realised that he needed to find his Lover, and discover if they had a child. He packed his things and hurriedly left the forest that had become his home for years, and set upon a new quest – to find the truth and speak his truth, that he had never stopped loving her and would cherish the product of their love.

Patience without Prejudice

On his new quest, the fool encountered a Blind Woman listening to three sisters. The sisters lost their mother very early; and fought all their lives. Because one was always left out, and in fear of being the one who was left out, two sisters would always form an alliance against a third. Though it changed like the seasons as to whom, one was always isolated.

The sisters' father had died, leaving them his possessions, but without a will. The eldest sister had always managed the household and the family, including the money, and resented the responsibility. The youngest sister had always made the peace and resented her responsibility. The middle sister had always worked hard and resented the lack of reward. Each pleaded her case with deep emotion, and long-held feelings of hurt.

The Blind Woman, whose name was Justice, listened patiently and without prejudice. She listened to find out what solution would be fair and impartial. She knew, that no matter what her advice would be, that it would not please any sister completely. She understood that each sister would have to accept that she would not get her way.

Each sister had contributed to the wellbeing of the family. But, equally, each sister had contributed to her family's fracture. By not allowing her younger sisters to take some responsibility (financial or otherwise), the eldest sister became rigid and controlling. By always giving in to her older sisters and not standing up for herself, the youngest enabled their manipulations to become entrenched, and was constantly fearful of their reprisals and rejections. And by always trying to get attention, the middle sister seemed golden on the outside, but was constantly fearing that her sisters would stab her in the back. Neuroticism, anxiety, and paranoia. Such sorrow; left unshared and uncomforted.

The Blind Woman knew that these sisters would never truly love themselves because they had not learned to love one another. The people into whom they had grown were ugly on the inside, even if they were beautiful on the outside (and they were).

The Blind Woman wondered how to lead these sisters to love themselves and each other. She thought about holding their father's possessions in trust, so that they would have to work together to earn their release. Too controlling.

She wondered about giving all their father's possessions to charity, so they would have nothing to fight over. Hmmm.

JUSTICE DECIDED TO GET ANOTHER PERSPECTIVE.

She found a tree and climbed it, and then dangled herself over a branch by the knees, and then by her feet, and then – dangling by one single ankle.

Because she was blind, she couldn't see the world as anyone else could; but she was able to see her inner world, and this gave her a special wisdom. Dangling upside-down allowed the blood in her head to pool in her cerebrum and flood her frontal cortex with oxygen and glucose. She was able to think of something far better!!

With joy in her discovery, it seemed as though she danced off the tree-branch! The fool, transfixed by all he saw, imagined the Blind Woman flying, dancing, and swimming instead of dangling upside-down from the branch by one ankle – each time he moved, his view changed and so too did his interpretation of Justice. Changing his perspective, changed his mind as much as the Blind Woman's change in perspective enlightened her mind.

She leapt toward the three sisters, and said with impartial clarity:"Your desire for your father's love has drained you all of what makes you lovable. You have each become neurotic, anxious, and paranoid. In small amounts, these are not a problem. But you all have these afflictions and need professional help. My plan is this – sell your father's possessions, and with the money, pay for professional help to overcome your fears and insecurities. Get the viewpoints of others. Collect strategies to cope. Find ways to relate peacefully with one another. Continue to do this for one year, using your inheritance to pay for the professional help, and to pay for a gathering each week in which you three come together and express gratitude for your father's generosity. At the end of the year, host a celebration and invite everyone you know. Enjoy the fruits of your labours. Be grateful for the love of your sisters. Glow in love."

The fool saw that this was hard news to take, and the sisters argued with Justice for some time. Eventually, they understood that her solution was indeed impartial and fair. Eventually, they relented and agreed to the suggestion.

The fool, impressed, planted two seeds here, because he learned two valuable lessons. The first lesson was to wait until all the facts are delivered before making a decision. The second lesson was, that if you want a situation to change, you either change the situation or you change yourself – you can't expect someone else to change it for you – and this requires a change in perspective.

On the ground in the dirt, the fool drew the Blind Woman dangling from the tree-branch by one ankle. He walked around his picture. From one place, she looked like she was dangling upside-down and she could have been an acrobat practising a trick. From another place, it seemed like she was floating serenely on her back. From another place, she looked like she swam forwards in freestyle, like she meant to get somewhere quickly as though she were saving a drowning man or herself. And, from yet another angle, she was happily dancing or leaping or reaching up to pluck something from above.

The fool realised that if you don't change your perspective, then everything stands still, suspended. If nothing changes, then nothing changes! Whether you like it or not, when you're feeling stuck like this, it's time to rest or meditate or pray. These are the times for an epiphany!

When you change your perspective (viewpoint; mindset; approach; belief; value; thoughts about a situation or person, or yourself), you reveal the connections and solutions that previously eluded you. Who is floating? Who is suspended? Who is practising? Who is preparing? Who is swimming? Who is saving? Who is dancing? Who is reaching? Who is leaping? You are.

Chapter 3:
A new perspective

Suddenly, he saw that the seeds he planted had sprouted and grown.

Had he been there that long? He remembered running. He remembered wanting to find the High Priestess to tell her what he discovered. She would understand! This was such a momentous discovery! Changing perspective changes the situation and it changes me!! Such liberation!!! Such power!!! It's so fantastic and yet so simple!

He ran and ran, and then suddenly found the little copse of trees where he had planted some of his first seeds. The Emperor and the Empress were nowhere to be found now and were maybe long-gone, but the trees were large and strong, and bore fruit. There must have been hundreds of apples hanging heavily from the branches, and many more on the ground nestled in thick green grass.

The fool took a bite of a ripe and juicy apple straight from one tree, and happily lay down in the shade of another.

The fool looked up through the branches, at the blue skies and puffy white clouds, and thought about the young lad he once was. When he came here, naïve and innocent, he learned valuable lessons. Had he implemented what he learned? He certainly planted his seeds in gratitude, and they provided for him over all these years. Some had turned into trees like these above him, while others had become crops of grain, flowers and vegetables. So many and so much that others could certainly benefit.

[RE]BIRTH

The blue skies turned dark with sunset, and the stars began to twinkle above him. The grass beneath his head felt soft and secure.

The fool pondered the Universe, the changes he had witnessed over the years; the way life (despite some of his best efforts) just did not stay the same. He realised his own transformation. He was older now, to be sure, but his transformation was more – was deeper – than that. He had travelled far and wide, and had even accumulated many things along the way – trinkets and mementos of a life lived. What was worth keeping? Only the memories, and the love.

And with that, he fell into a deep sleep.

HE DREAMED OF A WOMAN MAKING THE IMPOSSIBLE WITH THE IMPROBABLE.

In his dream, the fool saw a woman with two cups, standing above a creek. She would place mystical substances in one cup and consider how to mix them with the liquid in the other, without blowing everything up! This was dangerous work, but important too. She looked straight at him, and, meeting his gaze, said "The trick is in knowing how much is too much, and how much is too little. It's so fine a line between the two, and I've been experimenting for such a long time".

The fool realised her determination was tempered with gentleness, and he was intrigued. He asked her for her name, and she said "Temperance". So apt!! She said that it was time to try again, and to stand back, "You might want to put these on", and she handed him protective goggles and earmuffs, as well as a crisp white lab coat. He put them on; and watched in fascination.

Temperance announced, "Attempt 137", and poured the contents of the two cups into the creek. It bubbled and gurgled, and began to expand. The fool was glad he was standing back, because the creek widened and deepened, becoming a river that flowed swiftly past him. Before he knew it, Temperance was out of sight, beyond the extremes of the river she had created.

The fool awoke, and in a clearing near the first three trees, he dug some holes and planted his apple core from last night together with another seed and nourished them with water from the stream nearby. His lesson, here, was to always temper his determination with gentleness. He planted for the future and felt gratitude for this lesson, and for his happy return to familiar realms.

He stood, whereupon, the Empress and the Emperor walked toward him and embraced their dear old friend. They walked into the castle and showed him back to the beautiful room where he once stayed before. He bathed, put on clean clothes and joined them for dinner. And there she was, his Lover!

It seemed he was rooted to the spot; shackled as it were, to the sight of her.

She was as young and as beautiful as the first moment he saw her. Was this some trickery? They ate the most delicious dinner and drank more wine than ever before, laughing and telling the stories of their lives. He had forgotten how comfortable this castle was, with soft silks and cashmeres, with ample couches and cushions. He revisited the glittering grandeur and the seductiveness of all the sensual delights of being here, and after dinner was over and all retired to their rooms, he went to her bed.

They made love like never before. All the years that had passed seemed not to make a difference. Their passions were undiminished. He kissed tenderly every pore of her skin, every hair on her precious head. He took her repeatedly, urgently, lustfully. He held her down, palms pressing palms, and looking straight into her eyes, he showed her the man that he'd become.

They slept in the moments between, and into the morning. When the sun's rays warmed their naked bodies, they awoke entwined in each other's legs and arms. His face was buried deep into the crook of her neck and surrounded by hair, sweetly scented with apple blossoms. In that moment, he thought, "I have everything I need", and he nestled evermore deeply.

She woke and realised that while she needed to be elsewhere, she was right where she wanted to be. She had long-dreamed of this time, when he loved her completely and without restraint. She had fought the urge to run after him when he left, and she wept bitter tears in her sorrow and loneliness. As much as she understood his need to leave, she also knew that she was partly his reason to go. She accomplished with love, what he could not, no matter how determined he was. That bruised his ego, and he could not find a way past it.

Now, she lay quietly thinking about all that had happened and that could have been. She rolled over to face him, and looked lovingly into his eyes, wanting to tell him the words she rehearsed so many times.

Chapter 4:
Shock

Suddenly the world shook.

They got up, and naked, ran out of the room before everything crumbled behind them. The crashing of walls was deafening; the booming of the roof falling to the ground reverberated right through them. They searched for any other survivors, frantically clutching at debris and flinging it into the air to pull them out from under the rubble.

The devastation was total. The castle, obliterated. The fool and his Lover managed to find the Empress and Emperor, who were glad that all their many children except the youngest were in their own homes and away from this explosive destruction and danger, and that their littlest, the twin boys, were safe in their arms.

The Lover, though, was frantic. There were two more children who were missing. A little younger than the twin boys, these were twin girls. Where were they?? The fool stayed calm and suggested using pullies and ropes to haul the bigger rubble away; to use tubes to listen for hidden voices. Together, they worked tirelessly into the night to find those children, taking turns to dig up rubble and to rest.

All that was left, was what was important. Love. Each other.

[RE]BIRTH

THE NIGHT WAS DARK, UNTIL VENUS AND JUPITER APPEARED IN THE SKY.

The two brightest heavenly bodies lit the sky and illuminated where the little ones were. They saw the Lover; and cried "Mamma!"

In an instant, the fool knew. These little ones were his. With renewed determination, he tore through the rubble to retrieve them and scooped each into his arms so that both were embraced lovingly and equally. His Lover, too, wrapped her arms around them all, and finally, they were a family.

Together, they all went to the river and felt the cool water embrace their tired bodies. The Emperor and the Empress dipped their boys into the water and washed their faces, throwing them lovingly in the air and catching them. The fool and his Lover, too, dipped their girls in the water and twirled them around in orbits, creating whirlpools. All were safe, and each played happily in the cool of the river.

Eventually, they got out of the water and dried off, lying on the soft grass, under the fool's trees. The children chased each other, giggling and tickling; girls saying, "chase me" and boys replying, "too easy!" It was hard to tell them apart. It was only when they all came to flop down with their parents that you could begin to see the subtle differences. The ones who were boisterous and liked to climb trees had the bigger eyes. The ones who were quieter and liked to have one-on-one conversations with the grown-ups had deeper foreheads. Apart from those differences, the boys were as identical as the girls.

The fool realised that his Lover had a story; and asked her to tell him. She decided that she would tell them all.

THE LOVER HAD TO GO ON, WITHOUT KNOWING WHERE SHE WAS, WHO SHE WAS, OR WHAT TO DO NEXT.

She had loved her fool, and, let him go. She had hoped that she would see him again, and soon, but had deep fears that she would not. Regardless, she needed to keep the faith – in her fool, and in herself.

Sometimes, she thought she saw him, wandering through a forest or climbing a mountain. She would watch quietly until he disappeared. She desperately wanted to run after him, but told herself that when he was ready, he would come and find her. When she was lonely, it only added to her confusion. Darkness made it harder to discern dreams from nightmares. Sometimes, she was paralysed by fears that she would not be able to go on without him.

The months passed, and her belly grew. She had no idea what was happening. Her back ached and often, she felt completely alone. But sometimes, when the moon was full and lit the valleys and trees, twinkling on the river and making the sweet scent of the flowers even stronger, she felt completely at peace. On those nights, the Lover felt enveloped by benevolent beings, angels all around her guiding her on, showing her towards a place that she could call home.

On one of those nights, those softly starry moonlit nights, she came to a cave. Someone had been living there and had left bedding, soft and clean; but wasn't there then. There was a cup, a knife, a staff and a seed, as well as a cloth. She planted the seed outside the cave in homage to her fool, and collected water from a nearby stream, and lay down to rest for the night under the cloth.

Although alone, she wasn't lonely, for that night she gave birth to two beautiful baby girls. Somehow, she had known all along that she was pregnant and that there were two blessed spirits travelling with her. Her trust and intuition carried her on. And so she called her daughters, Faith and Hope, and thanked the Moon for showing her to this cave ~ this safe space for a mother and babes ~ and she gave thanks for the man who gave her these two beloved gifts.

She rested, and when she awoke the following morning, she met the Empress. Together, they walked with their broods back to the castle, and with the Emperor, took care of these four little blessings.

[RE]BIRTH

SO, WHAT WAS HIDDEN, WAS REVEALED.

In the intervening years, Hope and Faith played with the boys, Rafael and Michael. Each developed their own personality and drive. Each gave the others time to shine, and all encouraged each other to be optimistic and creative. They loved with the openness of children and the joy of friendship. When they looked upon one another these little ones saw the sun shining, and they smiled! They sang and warbled like birds, and they danced with blithe abandon!

Their parents were shining examples of warmth and generosity. They taught their children through their actions, using kind words and loving tones. Things could not always be good, but they could always support one another. Every year, the Lover would take her daughters to the river, to each plant a seed for Daddy, and that was why his first three trees were surrounded by a little forest of their own.

The fool suddenly sat up and looked around himself, and saw the trees and the saplings, planted by his daughters. He wept, feeling the need to put down roots, to build a home, and to show his family that he loved them dearly. He was compelled to look over his life and see that some reparation was due. He owed it to his Lover to be there for her, and he owed it to his children to support them to grow into the best people they could become. He realised that his past decisions had caused his Lover heartache and loneliness, and as he begged her forgiveness he offered her solace in his devotion. He acknowledged that his absence caused her desolation and fear, and he dedicated his undying commitment to her. Finally, he asked her what she wanted from him, to balance this karma; and she said simply, "your love, My Darling". She had loved him all these years; and had forgiven him even as he took his first step away from her newly-pregnant form. Now, he was here, and she was happy.

A PROPHET CHANGES THE WORLD.

One day the fool took his Lover to the cliff that started it all, together with Hope and Faith. His journey was complete, at least this part of his journey, and he was ready to share the next with them.

He found that he had grown in wisdom, not just because he had spent time alone, nor because he had shared himself with another. He shared his secrets with his family – that each step of life was an adventure that could lead to other souls and new discoveries, and all he had to do was be open to those experiences and then let them go. He remembered and recounted the lessons he had learned –

* You have everything you need (and a big part of that is your imagination).
* Listen to your intuition and learn discernment through experience and validation.
* Be welcoming and hospitable; include others in your life.
* Know where your home is (even if it's in your heart), and plan for the future.
* If God exists, then nothing is impossible.
* To make a wise choice, get the facts first.
* If you are determined to succeed, you need to know and organise your resources.
* Stand your ground when you must; but balance your drive with gentleness.
* Take time alone to think, meditate and pray ~ often.
* Be aware of life's cycles to know when to act, and when to step back; and understand that your actions will have consequences.
* Truth is impartial and fair (though not always pleasant).
* When stuck, take a different perspective and try to get the whole picture.
* Transformation entails life and death, discovery and liberation, accepting and letting go.
* Peace begins when you release expectations.
* Temper determination with patience; science with softness.

[RE]BIRTH

- If you feel trapped, ask "What is my role in this?". You have the keys to your own salvation.
- When everything seems lost, remember what's important.
- Relax, have fun, do what you need to heal.
- When you have to go on without a clue, trust in the benevolence of the heavens.
- Give life. Support growth. Radiate love. Be the example that children need and want.
- Karma will always catch up, with us all.
- When you reach a milestone, celebrate! Enjoy! Share the moment with others!

And he realised the one lesson he started with …Just trust.

With that, he tied the cloth he started with to the staff he carried all these years, and (knowingly) ran and leapt off the cliff, holding the ends of the rod as the cloth filled with air and lifted him off the ground.

As his family watched, he flew.

Part 2:
The Minor Arcana

In the Introduction, we talked about the Major Arcana and the Minor Arcana as "libraries" or "collections" of cards. We saw the Major Arcana as "the fool's journey" in Part 1. Did you resonate with the fool? Maybe you saw yourself as one of the other characters of the story? That's completely natural, because as we grow in wisdom, we **become** those other characters.

We do become the master or mistress of our own destiny! We trust our intuition, especially when we have those *A-ha!* moments in life. We are welcoming .. we offer sage advice .. we fall in love .. we learn from education, experience and introspection .. we listen and we teach .. we work with others .. we can be fair.

You have been on the fool's journey …. Now I invite you to explore your own life in more intricate beauty and savagery through the Minor Arcana. If you look at a regular deck of cards, you will see how it is similar to the Minor Arcana. In the Minor Arcana, we see four suits, like a regular card deck. Instead of hearts, spades, clubs and diamonds, the Minor Arcana has Cups (hearts), Swords (spades), Wands (clubs), and Pentacles (diamonds). Pentacles are sometimes called coins, too. Also, similar to a regular deck of cards, the Minor Arcana has numbered cards (Ace-10) and court cards (Princess or Page, Prince or Knight, Queen and King).

The tarot purists might not agree with what I suggest in this book, and I do apologise for that, but my aim is not about teaching tarot history or divination. Please remember that this book is more about self-discovery and understanding others; and has absolutely nothing to do with telling fortunes. Please try other books if that is what you seek. But I invite you (even urge you) to continue with this book, because you will deepen your own wisdom by reading on .. and it won't be burdensome, I promise!

But first, here is a little preamble to fit you into the Minor Arcana ….

When we are born, it's been debated, that a baby's first concept of self is that it is completely unaware of anyone else. It is, and there is nothing else (just like the fool!).As the baby grows, it becomes aware of others (and especially parents and other children). The baby starts to notice "agency" – who does what, who makes certain sounds, who responds if Baby cries. The baby starts to learn how to manipulate their environment: crying gets attention, attention can lead to cuddles and an improvement in physical feelings (like hunger and thirst). Eye contact can lead to attention too, as can smiling and laughing and cooing. Joint attention is one of the next steps, and (together with pointing) helps the baby to learn all sorts of useful stuff that they will use through their entire life!

This is a simple description of the beginnings of "theory of mind", a clunky jargonistic way of saying that we humans (and a few other animals) learn who we are in relation to others. Without it, we don't develop empathy. With it, we can flourish limitlessly. With too much, we can go off the rails occasionally. Would you believe, I designed a test around this concept for my PhD? That was a lifetime ago! But, back to what I was saying ….

We develop social competency and even social intuition with increasing experience, and parents can help this process along by doing a few basic things:

* Quietly read age-appropriate stories with your child every night around bedtime;
* Talk about characters in stories, in terms of how they feel;
* If you can, have more than one child (four is a pretty good number, and more is even better) or encourage your children to spend lots of time with their cousins and neighbouring children;

- If you can't have many children, try to send your child to a good preschool;
- Do your best to ensure your child has emotional intelligence and empathy before they start school (this is not associated with their age, but their maturity).

Now, I have plenty of amazing and lovable friends who have no siblings, so please don't worry if you can't tick off everything! I actually think the last item on the list is the best advice (though all items have research to back them up). I like a few other things too … like making good eye contact and smiling at your child, making them feel treasured, cherishing your time with them, making time for fun and adventure with them. And I love The Power of Chores …

When I was growing up (in a big family of nine children), we had a roster to do the chores after dinner (stacking up the dishes, washing, drying, putting things away, and sweeping the floors). That way, we all contributed to the family's wellbeing. We also had a list of "pay-jobs" which included doing the ironing (tablecloths etc), washing floors, vacuuming carpets, dusting, polishing the car, cleaning the venetian blinds and windows …. So many jobs! *And so much opportunity … doing housework gives children a chance to learn to do something useful and to a standard (**self-efficacy**), to negotiate a pay-rate, to earn some cash and develop independence (**self-agency**), and start to have faith in their own abilities (**self-confidence**).*

As my siblings and I got older, we would have celebrations on our patio, where it became very noisy! When we ran out of mugs and spoons, someone would go to the kitchen to wash, and someone else would follow to dry, and there, we would discover what was really going on in each other's life at that time. Some of the deepest conversations you can have with another human are over dirty dishes (even when you gently but humorously return a washed mug because it doesn't meet your standard of "clean"!!).

The point is – if you have a relationship that is struggling, you can always try sharing the housework. Not nagging or doling out jobs! Sharing.

The fool and his Lover agree to spend one hour every Saturday morning on housework. One cleans the bathroom, while the other collects the trash and recycling, and puts them out in the bins. One dusts, while the other takes the scraps out to the chickens and cleans up after the dog. And no-one complains about "standards"!!

Next door, the Empress and her sons agree to spend one hour during the week on tidying the sons' bedroom, so they're allowed to play with their friends on the weekend. The Empress agrees that if the sons put their dirty clothes in their hamper each day (instead of on the floor), she will wash them and return them to a specified place in their room, so they can put them away where they can find them.

One of the other things I appreciated growing up, was this little trick: Parent sets rules. Parent sets consequences for breaking rules (where consequences are relevant to that particular child), and parent communicates the rules and consequences to the child clearly. When child breaks the rules, the parent is consistent in meeting the consequences.

Without rules, consequences and consistency, children will develop anxiety. This is just as surely as if they experience adversity or trauma. Look at the people you know. The grown-ups you know who have fears and phobias will probably have a time in their childhood when they didn't know the rules because things were too unclear or too chaotic.

This feels a bit like sermonising, which is uncomfortable for me, and I apologise if it is for you too. But I wanted to set the scene for Part 2 – because this is where we use the Minor Arcana to understand our own personal development, and our relationships with other people.

I mentioned the four suits earlier – Cups, Swords, Wands, Pentacles. Think about each representing a part of your life. I'd invite you to get a book (especially a nice book) in which to write notes as you read further. If you started drawing your Major Arcana from Part 1 in a nice book, you might like to continue depositing your impressions of the Minor Arcana there too.

Think about the Cups as your family telling you messages about your love relationships. Love has many forms, including family, romance, friendship and even business/colleagues and partnership. You might want to list (and/or draw) some people who are important to you right now, and some people from your past who were influential. Cups are emotional and relational! My mother used to say to me when I was seeing someone romantically, "Does he treat you well? Does he make you happy?". As far as I'm concerned, that's a pretty good test of what love is. Think about yourself as The Empress: what makes you feel hospitable and affectionate?

Now think of the Swords as your intellect telling you messages about what you need to learn and master, as well as what you could teach and communicate (and how best to get your own message across). You might want to list (and/or draw) all the schools you attended, the subjects that inspired you, and the educational milestones to which you have aspired. Swords are about your aspirations for knowledge and wisdom, and about your intellectual achievements. The lesson with the swords is that if you get bored, ever, you need to continue learning something. And one of the best ways to learn is to teach someone who just "doesn't get it". Think of yourself as The Magician: what do you have, and what do you need?

Now, it's time to think about work, because the Wands are about occupation and even vocation. Which jobs have empowered you? What work was fulfilling? When did you feel like you could make a difference? You might like to write down what you put into your employment, and next to it, what you gained from it. Another way to think about the Suit of Wands is to imagine you are at a party and someone asks you "what do you do?". What labels do you use? Some of the labels I've used include a project manager, remedial massage therapist, Reiki practitioner, mental health researcher, scientist, workshop facilitator, measurable change agent ... you get the picture! But more importantly, this is how you spend your time. Do you squander your time watching television, internet shopping or playing online games? This is indolence, and you could be having a much better (and happier life) doing something else. Think about yourself as The Emperor: what is important to you in building for the future?

Finally, we turn to the Pentacles and consider community and contributions. Where do you feel you belong? How do you contribute? What are you doing for future generations? Here's where you might like to think of the seeds that you plant, the people you nurture, and the way in which you lead others. Think about yourself as The High Priestess: what is missing from your life, and what gives you a sense of purpose?

Chapter 5:
Kings and Queens

You've considered the four suits and how they relate on a general level to your life; now let's turn to your personal development.

If you have a deck of tarot cards, please put them aside because you will not use your imagination as much if they are in front of you. Instead, you might like to think of people that embody the qualities we've just mentioned. Who is an emotional person? Who is intellectual? Who is industrious? Who brings people together? Who is foreign? Who has never left their home-town? Who is loyal? Who loves to argue? Write it all down and better yet, draw them! These are great insights into who you are ….

As you start to draw your impressions, think about certain attributes (positive and negative) that reflect you in certain situations, but also represent others. Let's begin with the Kings. Start by thinking about your own aspirations in relation to your father (or father-figure, maybe a grandfather, uncle or step-father). Think about him in his different relationships. Think about him in his purest and highest, best form, and how you reflect those special qualities now. Think about your father (or father-figure) when his aspirations were frustrated, when his hopes were dashed, when his dreams shattered. How do you resemble his reactions and responses?

We should probably stipulate here, that "reactions" are those gut-driven actions, while "responses" are more measured and considered.

Think about your father or father-figure in terms of Cups (family, romance, friendships, business partnerships and close colleagues); in terms of Swords (education, life experience, communication style, feelings toward learning something new and speaking in front of others); in terms of Wands (work, a sense of vocation, fulfillment in one's occupation, promotion and loss of employment); and in terms of community (club, politics, neighbourhood, sense of belonging, contribution to society, planning for future generations). You might like to draw four pictures, one for each suit, representing your father(-figure) in his four main roles as father and partner, as learner and teacher, as worker (or employer), and as a contributor to his community.

When my father passed away, other siblings prepared and delivered his eulogy. They were heartfelt reminiscences but very different from my own memories. You see, my siblings were all older than me, so they remembered Dad a little differently. They were raised in the fifties and sixties. Regardless of how Dad felt about it, it was expected that naughty children were chastised with a smack, slap, strap or belting. I was raised in a more compassionate time, and I recall being an infant at the dinner table, with my brothers and sisters complaining that I was "spoiled" because Dad never smacked me. It never occurred to them that as the youngest I was learning from all their mistakes and not making them, ergo, I was not naughty and therefore did not deserve to be punished! (Or, not!).

To please them, Dad called me from my corner of the big table to his, got me to lay over his legs, and he gave me one quick slap on my covered behind. He stood me up and with tears in my eyes, I asked, "What did you do that for?", to which he replied, "Just in case". Apart from that one moment, I was never physically chastised by my father, ever. And I never wanted to be. I couldn't bear the thought of making him angry, because I didn't want him to be anything but happy. As I grew older, I often had occasion to spend time talking just with Dad, about mental health and severe mental illness, politics, investing in shares, saving, buying and maintaining a car ... I remember one particular gentleman would come to visit my parents, and he had been diagnosed with schizophrenia from his early twenties. One day, he was fast-approaching a psychotic episode, and calmly my father was able to bring him back to the edge of reason and the tranquillity of normalcy. Dad had such a great intuition for that sort of thing, even though he wasn't a psychologist or psychiatrist. I learned a great deal from Dad, not just because he was a fountain of knowledge (which he was), but because he recognised in me the potential and hunger to learn. From early on, he treated me as he thought we all should be treated, with respect and love.

Now, this exercise is about you ... so try it again, but thinking about you in relation to your father(-figure) and all his different roles. You might like to draw your pictures again, this time with you as the "King" of each domain.

Yes! This is different to any "tarot" book you've ever read! Remember that we're exploring your experiences of –

* Caring and Nurturing ... Cups
* Learning and Communicating ... Swords
* Working and Devoting ... Wands
* Belonging and Contributing .. Pentacles

Now, try the exercise with the Queens. Think of your mother or mother-figure(maybe a grandmother, aunt or step-mother).Think this time about your own aspirations in relation to your mother (or mother-figure). Think about her in her different relationships. Think about her in her purest and highest, best form, and how you reflect those special qualities now. Think about your mother (or mother-figure) when her aspirations were frustrated, when her hopes were dashed, when her dreams were shattered. How do you resemble her reactions and responses? Remember - "reactions" are gut-driven, while "responses" are more measured and considered.

Think about your mother or mother-figure in terms of Cups (family, romance, friendships, business partnerships and close colleagues); in terms of Swords (education, life experience, communication style, feelings toward learning something new and speaking in front of others); in terms of Wands (work, a sense of vocation, fulfillment in one's occupation, promotion and loss of employment); and in terms of community (club, politics, neighbourhood, sense of belonging, contribution to society, planning for future generations). Try drawing four pictures representing your "mother(-figure)" in her four main roles of mother and partner, student and teacher, worker/employer, and contributor to her community.

Now, think about you in relation to your mother(-figure) and all her different roles, and draw yourself as the "Queen" of the four suits.

After my mother died, a priest talked about her at church the following weekend, and used the words "social justice". I had never thought of either of my parents in that sense. They were Mum and Dad to me, wife and husband to each other, friends and neighbours and members of a church community. What I forgot was how much they both contributed to the wellbeing of others, through working in various charities and not-for-profit organisations, and quietly donating to charities that cared for people who were poor and homeless, including young people. These two words, "social justice" reminded me of how my beloved parents were part of a wider community and worked towards making things better for my family and others. And let's face it, they made a lot of troubled times in my life so much better .. thankfully!

Now that we've become acquainted with the Kings and Queens, let's turn to the children and teenagers of the Minor Arcana.

Chapter 6: The little children of the Minor Arcana

Show me the baby!!

I love babies. I describe myself as having ADOB (Attention Deficit Oh Baby!). The baby is the Ace (Ace, Ace, Baby!)! Remember the baby we talked about earlier? That baby is the spark of wonder and the promise of limitless possibility. As the baby grows, it becomes aware of others and it's relationship to those others. But first, it just is. The baby, the Ace of everything, is the fool; innocent, naïve and needing to trust in others to survive (without even knowing it). The fool is beautiful and uncomplicated, and embodies all that is wonderful in humanity. That's how I feel about babies.

But there's more to it. Remember how we talked about the suits? The aces of the suits are the sparks of each part of our life. They are about joy, passion, energy, clarity, intuition, and imagination. They are about the start. The aces are about **being, perceiving, trying**, and **committing**. Think, for a moment, which of those four verbs relates to which suit! I might tease you and suggest we'll come back to that!

Think back to a time when you fell in love at first sight, to discovering a job that seemed perfect just for you, to seeing a course as your ticket to bigger and better things, or realising that you wanted (needed?) to give something back to society or leave a legacy for others. Those are the moments that describe the aces. That

sudden quickening in the heart that heralds something new and exciting! Now is a great time to open your journal or book so you have two blank pages. Draw a horizontal line through the middle of them so you have four quadrants. Start the habit of identifying which quadrants (for you) are Cups, Swords, Wands and Pentacles, remembering that:
* Caring and Nurturing ... Cups (**being**)
* Learning and Communicating ... Swords (**perceiving**)
* Working and Devoting ... Wands (**trying**)
* Belonging and Contributing .. Pentacles (**committing**)

Do you like what I just did? I snuck those verbs in there while you might not have been paying attention! You might look back and wonder why?? Think about it for a moment. What is the most important part of each? **Being** in the moment, **being** together, **being** present (ahh, you're getting it!) is what is important in relationships. Learning and communicating won't happen if nothing new is **perceived**! Nothing gets done if nobody **tries** to do it to start with ... and we're never truly part of a community until we choose to **commit** (we join a club, attend a sermon, open our mouths to sing along ...).

Sorry, did you think I was going to talk about small children for the rest of the book? No, I'm all about the allegory. And the allegory of the aces is the spark that starts the fire. Remember those four quadrants? Please take a little time to fill them with examples of your own "Aces From The Past", and repeat overleaf with your present aces and your future aces.

Do you see a pattern? Does the pattern repeat in one particular quadrant? Is it because you really love the feeling, so you keep repeating something; or because there's a lesson you haven't learned, and the Universe keeps sending you back for repeat classes? I won't judge; this is your trip afterall! Turn the pages to a new blank page and write down your own thoughts and impressions, as well as any new behaviours to which you might like to commit. I hope you feel the excitement that I feel while I'm writing this, because for me, this is such a special part of your transformation trip! Understanding this single step is a massive key to unlocking your life! In fact, I would encourage you to sleep on it tonight. Have a notepad and pencil next to you, because I have a feeling you will get many more insights before morning breaks! As my Mum would say each evening at bedtime, "Goodnight, sweet dreams, and God bless you".

TERRIBLE TWOS (NOT REALLY, NOT TERRIBLE AT ALL)

I hope you slept well last night, but that you also had lots of insights into your life. Go ahead, add them to your journal and see the patterns, the slip-ups, the whoopsie-daisies, the happy coincidences, the serendipity ...

I love serendipity, to the point that I named my second business "The Centre of Serendipity". For me, it means "where hard work and opportunity collide; where the impact is felt". When I describe it to someone, I sometimes smack my hands together (very hard and loudly), because I love the collision and impact of it. "It's where the impact is felt."

Hopefully you are getting the sense of duality I'm trying to impart here. Hard work AND opportunity .. The Twos of the Minor Arcana relate to duality. I saw a beautiful TED-talk in which the late Emily Levine said, "reality comes into being through an interaction". That is so exquisite. The interaction can be a synergy, or it can be a slow-burn, or a rubbing against a grain ...it can be the duality of evidence and intuition, of learning and instinct, of closeness and separation. So, this is where we ask ourselves, "Who lifts me up and makes me happy?", "Who empowers me to speak up and makes me feel confident?", "Who gives me independence and material resources?", "Who inspires me to make a difference for the future?". You might like to draw your impressions in your journal, and draw as many that come to you. Don't hold back. But try, if you can, to draw them in the quadrants that fit your suits.

The flipside, of course, is your impact on others. Who do you raise up? Who do you encourage? Who do you make safe and secure?

Who do you inspire to make the world a better place? We all have a right to respect and dignity, and a responsibility to remember that about each other. Sure, we make mistakes, but we keep on trying.

THREE IS A CROWD

You might find that there is another side to your relationships here, and it especially comes into play when there is a third party involved, because the third party can bring jealousy, envy, greed, and a fear of missing out. Who drags you down and makes you sad? Who makes you quiet or expects you to keep dark secrets? Who takes your things, or drains you of wealth and security? Who bleeds your dreams of a better world? These are the people whose influence you might like to evaluate carefully, because they might not be the channels to your higher power. When you draw those people in those interactions with you, remember the sorrow, frustration, impotence and hopelessness that you feel around these people. You might like to learn how to be (safely) more respectfully assertive around them. I'm not saying you should, I'm just saying you might like to learn. Or, you might like to quietly leave.

Now, it's time to shift the focus onto you. Over whom do you have an unhealthy influence? Who is the oyster muscle to your grain of sand? Who is weakened by your tone, words, actions or presence? Draw these interactions into your journal too, because this is where you learn how things have unravelled, and how you can become a better person. Draw those scenes of others weeping because of their interactions with you, and consider how you could have handled those situations differently. Commit to a new version of yourself, and draw how you could be in the future.

The fool had a nightmare. In it, he overheard the Empress yelling at his Lover, saying "You don't ever consider me! You never think about my feelings!" The Empress sounded so angry, and there were other people everywhere around them. He felt so badly for his Lover, but was powerless to help her. After a while, he watched as she and the Empress parted company. His Lover needed time to heal. She felt each word deeply, and was wounded. The fool tenderly put his arms around his Lover, and she told him what had happened. She said that the Empress had been upset by one of the older children, and when she recounted her story, she spoke as though the Lover was the person at fault.

The fool was confused, because he had heard the Empress repeatedly use the word "you" instead of her child's name, so it looked and sounded as though the Lover had caused the Empress's pain, instead of the offending family-member. It felt, to the fool, as though the Empress was angrily stabbing the Lover repeatedly with her harsh words. The Lover said, "I know she doesn't mean it, but it is hurtful; she forgets to consider my feelings because she is so caught up in being hurt herself. She doesn't realise how much her words hurt me. I retreat somewhere alone, and I meditate to wrap myself in a cocoon of white healing light, so I can heal".

In those times, the "third person" can be the powerlessness that the fool experienced, or the disappointment the Lover felt in not being heard. But it's also the unmet expectations of all. You can see how this "third person" comes into the picture here. When you love someone, you have expectations that they will treat you lovingly, and sometimes, that isn't what happens. But it's not just with people we love! Often, it's our colleagues, neighbours and strangers.

Years ago, I had my eye on a colleague and it seemed that he felt the same about me but wasn't ready to say so. We got along famously. That is, other people at work could see we got along! But there was one, who was a really lovely person, who also got along with him. In my jealousy, I said something horrible to her, in front of others. She was so gracious about it, bless her, but I was mortified. The "third person" here, was jealousy. For ten years, I carried the guilt and shame, even though she forgave me. And so, guilt and shame could have become the "third person" in my subsequent relationships. These are the kinds of situation we're talking about here, and it's a good opportunity for us all to be honest about our horrible times that we'd rather forget. Draw yours, and write about them; and decide how to - avoid them happening again, protect yourself, or how you can heal yourself afterwards.

Awesome Foursome versus the Gang of Four

The fours are all about feeling part of a group, and about making a pact that lasts. So, what happens when you get with your tribe? Again, think about you but in the positive light. Because you no longer feel alone, you are an inspiration for love, intellectual pursuit, vocational endeavour, and community contribution. You are also part of a tribe and they sustain you. They give you power, confidence, a voice! This doesn't have to just be a group of four people, it can be that feeling that everything is falling into place. You have the home, car, partner and job. You have health, home, prosperity and posterity. You have faith, hope, generosity and love. Draw in your journal those situations in which you have felt (or feel now) that you are part of something special, something bigger than just you. For me, it has been on retreat or after mass, with other like-minded souls, talking about faith. For others, it might be joining a club or a political party, or a group on social media. I remember fondly the times that I've sung around the piano with my siblings, or the night my sister and I sang "Pearly Shells" in perfect harmony while doing the dishes together. Dad commented how well we sounded! Another time was my first experience of white-water rafting on the Murray River, paddling through the wash over rocks in a Grade 5 rapid! You feel indomitable.

Raphael, Michael, Hope and Faith were playing among the apple and lemon trees near the river. Faith started singing "Lemon tree, very pretty, and the lemon flower is sweet, but the fruit of the poor lemon is impossible to eat", and then Hope joined in, a little after, so that the song became a round. The boys joined in and before long, they warbled in harmonies and played with different voices until they exhausted themselves. It was so perfect!

There is always a flipside, though. The fours tell us about how we are when we're in a gang. And that means, what is the worst you have experienced or caused because you ran with the wrong crowd? What's the worst that has happened because you were employed by the wrong company? What are the bad things that happened because you learned the wrong things?

Flying Fives

What patterns do you see? Do you see that you have had opportunities to learn along the way? The Fives of the Minor Arcana are about the balance between learning and teaching. When we are inexperienced, we need to learn and to practice. When we are experts, we have a responsibility to teach and mentor, as well as supervise and sponsor. There is always a blurring of the lines between the junior and senior selves; a competition between the old lion and the young contender. I remember working for a man, who brought together staff and students from around the globe, to work on mental health research projects. He was a clever man, and rightly proud of his achievements, with a good sense of humility (as opposed to modesty). He had another man working in his team, who was about to complete his PhD. My boss pulled me aside one day, and said that when a person finishes their PhD, they are expected to go away and work for someone else or establish their own lab. But my colleague had other ideas. He, too, was a clever man! He argued with my boss, often in front of the rest of the team, like the young lion challenging the older lion for the right to the pride. It was fascinating to witness (especially as they were both Leos!). This was a learning experience for both, and the teaching tool was competition. Instability could have ensued if my colleague had won the argument (another teaching tool). Change, conflict, growth, loss, disappointment, unwinnable arguments … these are the teachers that force us to grow.

So, now, think about those times that you have had "growing pains". You'll recognise the times: when you look back, you think "that was the worst time of my life", and the period just after will be "the happiest I've ever been". As I write this, I am in that happiest period. My difficult time took about a decade for me to wrestle with. I had started my PhD, and it had a couple of false starts followed by years of not knowing what I was supposed to do (because I expected that my supervisors would tell me, and teach me valuable research skills). Additionally, I had romantic issues (both lovely and terrible), issues with where I lived and worked, health scares, and the loss of my dear parents. It all collected in one foul swamp of challenges. For five years, although I had a great job, I didn't appreciate it fully because it wasn't how I imagined myself: I labelled myself a mental health researcher but was working in cancer, and hated the incongruency of it all. My identity and my sense of self did not match.

After those five years, I decided to resign and take some time off work. I just wanted to go with the flow, like the fool in the Major Arcana. I wanted to see where life would take me, and I was open to the Spirit of the Universe. In the first fortnight, I designed and published my first website, painted for the first time since I was 15 (that's over 30 years), and signed up for a business course. I redid my general First Aid Certificate and my Mental Health First Aid Certificate, and started allowing my creativity to just flow. For the first time in my life, I wrote a blog, and followed it up every month thereafter, finding inspiration in my daily life.

So, here, the job for you, is to consider those tough times and the teaching tools they brought, as well as the lessons you learned. For example, when I left a relationship that was constantly hurtful, I bought my first house and exiled myself there, realising that it was not only my sanctuary but my saviour. I no longer felt the need to be in a relationship: I was happy on my own. When my marriage ended, so too did my child-bearing capacity (menopause came to visit, and got comfortable). I used to be obsessed with marriage and motherhood, and now, it's not important to me anymore. I never used to be a pet-person (and I especially wasn't a dog-person), but I've fallen in love with my neighbour's puppy!

The point is: things change. They are often difficult and challenging, disappointing and disheartening. But they can herald better times. As much as I miss my parents, I can talk to them any time I like. I have a deep sense of them being with me and working for my wellbeing, and that's possibly because I've always been open to the spiritual side of life, but possibly too, because I am imaginative. I'd like to invite you now to think about those hard times; the times when you ran out of money, when your friend told your secrets, when you lost the love of your life, when you felt betrayed. When you draw in your journal, remember those quadrants if you can (Caring and Nurturing … Cups (being); Learning and Communicating … Swords (perceiving); Working and Devoting … Wands (trying); Belonging and Contributing .. Pentacles (committing)). Try to think about the way you felt in those times, the anger, frustration, impotence, sorrow, heartbreak. We'll come to the good times again soon, I promise. But for now, just accept that bad times happen, and they pass sooner or later. My rotten time went for 12 years in total (2006-2018), but there were lots of good times in there (including my wedding day).

What patterns do you see? Are you anxious in certain situations involving others? Do you have romantic courage? Are you confident in using your own wisdom and intuition? Have you suffered panic at the thought of continuing your education? Have you held back on giving to charity because there are so many, and you feel overwhelmed? I have a confession. I have experienced all these and more. Moreover, I am depicted in all the pictures described above. We all have the capacity to hurt and to heal, and sometimes it can be the exact same tone, word, action or presence, just a different context. The important things are to be aware, and to be genuinely sorry. It also helps to make amends when possible. I mentioned earlier how I said something horrendously mean to a colleague, and for the following decade, I did what I could to always provide professional support to her so that others would see how high my regard really was for that person.

So here, let's focus on the changes and challenges of your life: draw them, embellish them, make them shine. Because you – you – have grown from them! And you shine.

Sweet, Serene Sixes!

I mentioned earlier about the way life twists and turns from the downhill run to flying high in the clouds. We're flying now! These are the times when you found a solution to a vexatious problem, the wherewithal to buy your first home or your first overseas holiday, the first time you passed an exam or got a better mark in your university course. You work hard, and you keep on working harder until, wow! You did it! It's that sensational feeling of achievement. Once upon a time, I went white-water rafting with a friend from work and a bunch of her friends. I was petrified, because I wasn't a good swimmer. I kept thinking that I'd drown, or worse, embarrass myself. The guys sensed my fear! Once we had gone over some rapids and found ourselves in calm water, they threw me overboard! Eventually, they pulled me back in, after having had a good laugh. We have a saying in Australia (probably everywhere else too): "What's the worst that can happen?". Well, a lot worse could have happened, and didn't. And really, I wasn't embarrassed. It was fun and funny. The moral of the story is, the sixes show you that you come out the other end a survivor.

Have you ever had that gut feeling, and then the validation of your intuition? Have you experienced love at first sight? Have you discovered that the love of your life is not the type of person you thought you'd end up with (a great example is the rocker and his manager in the film, "Love Actually")? These are examples of the 6 of Cups.

Have you had to work on a mathematical or chemistry problem for school, and after working on it unsuccessfully for hours, you take the dog for a walk and, Boom! The answer hits you, like a lightning bolt. I like to describe those times as Einstein Moments. You have to put the hard work in, but you also need to walk away so the information has a chance to be filed away by your brain, and then retrieved in the way you need to use it: 6 of Swords.

Have you worked tirelessly for your boss, hoping that a promotion or raise will be offered to you but never getting either? After a while, you start a course and discover that you'd like a different job, or that you love your job and don't need the extra money or responsibility? Maybe the course gives you a newfound confidence to – out loud – ask for that raise and promotion! That's 6 of Wands.

So, what would 6 of Pentacles look like? Generosity. Needing or waiting for a hand-out, or a helping hand. Being able to help someone else. Having generosity in your heart, and it's born of caring. That's the 6 of Pentacles.

So, I invite you to think about those times when you have needed someone's help, and received it. It may have been help born of love (like a parent helping you to move house or a friend who brings you home from hospital); help born of intellect (like a tutor explaining a concept, or study-buddies helping you get a better mark than you ever have before); vocational help (maybe someone helping with your resume or a position); or it may be born of your sense of community (a scholarship or grant).

And now, think about the times when you have helped someone else, because you loved them, saw their potential, believed in them, or cared about their future.

You know what to do ... draw in your book. Embellish. Make those people and times glitter. Generosity makes life sparkle!

STICKY SEVENS

Imposter Syndrome. We all feel it! If we're not careful, it can really hold us back. The sevens are about how our imagination can take us down dark alleyways of self-deception, irksome avenues of illusion, sneaky back passages of gossip and innuendo: in short, misunderstanding. These things hurt.

The fool had another dream, in which he watched the family of the Emperor and the Empress after their deaths. One son felt that all the others received more from their parent's estate, and felt left out, forgotten, unheard. He felt isolated and unsupported, and even less loved by his parents! He knew that the estate was to be distributed equally, but individual items held more or less value according to their stories and personal significance. His mother's jewellery was distributed to his sisters while the Empress was still alive, but nothing went to the sons. While the parents were alive, they gave each of their offspring an amount of money to go towards their first home; each was a 10% deposit on the same kind of house close to the family home. Yet, the older children were adults when the twins were born, and so 10% deposits over time held vastly different values. It was confusing!

The fool was deeply troubled, because he felt compassion for this older son, but could see that he was missing a vital point. The Empress and the Emperor had worked hard for all they had; they had the right to do with their estate whatever they wished, and their wishes should be respected. They did all they could to ensure their estate was distributed fairly. Moreover, they did what anyone would do for someone they loved: their hearts, filled with generosity, would overflow with kindness each time they could see that one of their children was hurt or needed help. It's not about fairness; it's about love for your children, and respect for your parents. In his dream, the fool sat with his friend's bereaved son, and talked about this at length, ensuring that the younger man was heard, but also his mind put at ease.

So, what have you experienced? Have you felt like people at work laugh at you behind your back? Have you felt that a friend has told your secret? Have you felt that someone else got a job that should have been yours, but they had a personal relationship with the employer? Have you felt that no matter what anyone says, your politicians will do nothing to save the environment? Have you been jealous about someone having the relationship that you want, or the baby you can't seem to conceive? Do you feel like you are always being criticised, or that someone will discover you're a fraud and disclose your weaknesses? Has someone stolen your work, your intellectual

[RE]BIRTH

property, your honour? All these things might be true .. but they might not, too. How do you learn and practice discernment?

The sevens are all about when fear takes control. Have you ever noticed, that when you get worried or anxious, that everything seems bigger and worse? You have trouble sleeping and that makes you impatient and clumsy, and you feel like others are judging you. You feel like you are losing control!

You know, we all have times like these. You're not alone. You are so normal! The trick is, to be able to breathe through it and find your inner calm. You need to rest and recuperate. Keep calm and convalesce!

Just because you have never been able to meditate, doesn't mean you won't always be able to. Try it with me now. Breathe in. Breathe out. There! You just meditated! In fact, you've been meditating all your life; you probably didn't even know it. You're a star at meditating. Try it again, except this time, when you breathe in, hold it for just a millisecond longer before you breathe out. For something different, I like breathing in, holding, breathing out, and imagining the space between the out-breath and the next in-breath. There is a beautiful flow, and it gets better in nature. Near a beach or river, on a mountain, surrounded by trees, in a desert. Ahh, the serenity!

You might have noticed by now, that when we think about the odd-numbered tarots, we consider the challenges, and the even-numbered tarots are the lights at the end of the tunnels. You might be getting that rhythm that "this too shall pass", so that every time we settle on those challenging times, we always remember the good times that have followed (however small). So, for now, let's settle in to those times when you let your imagination get the better of you because of your fear. Remember that time you thought your friend told your secret? You were really worried that that would happen, and it didn't, because your friend loved you and treasured your trust and friendship. Remember that job you didn't get because someone else was earmarked for the role before it was advertised? You were meant for something better. And, yes, I've been there in all these stories and more. You'll come out stronger and wiser (you probably already have).

You know what to do here: draw your fears in cups of sorrow, holding daggers of betrayal, wielding wands of destruction, and raining down comets from distant dying stars. Weep if you need to, and then wrap yourself in a soft white cloak of strength and heavenly protection.

MATES WITH EIGHTS

So, what's the life you want? Can you visualise it? What needs to change before you have that life? Can you break those big changes down to tiny, manageable tasks that fit into an hour?

The eights are all about having courage. Not just any kind of courage either. Do you have the courage to dramatically alter your life for the better? Are you willing to make the sacrifices necessary to achieve those changes? What if you had to stand up to a bully, protect a victim of elder abuse, get between a paedophile and a child? Do you have that courage? What if it meant losing your job or your home? How do you know if the sacrifices are worthy of your causes?

Once upon a time, when the High Priestess was young, she desperately wanted marriage and motherhood. A man with beautiful children came along, just after she had seen him in a dream. Her dream included his full name, as well as the names of his children, ex-wife and ex-parents-in law, so she thought he must be "The One". He pursued her relentlessly, which she thought was a sign that he loved her. She wanted marriage in a church; he never wanted to get married ever again. One day, he proposed! In public! She agreed, and moved in with him. Soon after, she discovered that he was an abusive man. She worried about his children, but his abuse was focussed toward her. It was mostly verbal, trying to make her feel like she was useless. She knew otherwise. Eventually, she decided that the children already had a great mother, and that it was undignified for the High Priestess to stay in the relationship. She left. As much as she loved those children, and it broke her heart to leave them, she knew that the sacrifice was worth the cause: her safety was more important than her dream to be a mother. By the time she left, he had hit her face twice, and subjected her to intercourse without consent countless times; and she had attempted leaving three or four times before. This time, her escape plan was more canny, and a little sneaky, because this time she did not return to her parents' like before, but she went somewhere else. And that place became her sanctuary.

Have you ever been in a situation that is "between a rock and a hard place"? You're "damned if you do and damned if you don't". You think that you should persevere, but your heart tells you it's time to try something different. I've just told you about a separation, but the courage you need might be for a union. Marriage takes courage! Allowing someone to live with you, when you've had the house to yourself for years, takes courage. Starting a business, employing staff for the first time, transforming your business from sole trader to company – all take courage.

Courage, on the other hand, has it's own needs. Courage needs information. It needs calculation and collaboration, combination and evaluation, separation and re-evaluation. Courage takes both science and art; evidence and intuition. You need to feel that what you're about to do will work out. A good example has been my second business (my first worked out, but my parents were alive then, and I had them to fall back on). I left a good job to go on what I called "Transformation Retreat". It was blissful. I took time for me. My house was clean, I wrote, I painted, I created! I used parts of my brain that had remained untouched for decades. And they still worked! But it took courage: a belief that everything would work out. My business takes so much of what I've learned over the years, and turns it into a constant creative process that's fun; and I get to spend much of my life meeting interesting people and hearing fascinating stories. I'm constantly inspired so I never run out of material for my blogs (though I try very hard to limit them to a monthly publication schedule so there are not too many). Life is good! The sacrifice is worth the cause!

So, what about you? Have you ever had to stand up for yourself or someone you care about? Have you stopped traffic to get to a rider who has flown off their motorbike? Have you been the first in the romantic relationship to say, "I love you", or the person to tell a co-worker that if they don't improve their behaviour they will lose their job? Have you ever had to start over, romantically, socially, vocationally, or had to move home? These are typical of the eights …. Try drawing them, and show how big your heart was; give it colour and round it out so it's as three-dimensional as you can make it. Because, your heart really would have been huge when you committed to change! And beating like mad!

Nearly There, Nines

Have you ever felt that you were nearly there, but you needed that one last push (shove) up the staircase of life? You're there! What are you hoping for? It's within reach! What are you working towards? You're going to get it! Just a few words of warning though, "be careful what you wish for". Sometimes, we strive so hard for something (or someone) and we are disappointed with the outcome. Just know that wishes are granted, and prayers are answered, but not always in the ways we want or in guises we recognise. I wanted marriage and motherhood, and I got it! But certainly not how I imagined it. And it ended.

Maybe you've lost sleep over all the things on your to-do list, or you're exhausted from always trying so hard. Maybe you're a perfectionist (stop it!!). Maybe you're too busy doing everything yourself because you don't trust someone else to help you (remember what I said earlier about self-agency, self-efficacy, and self-confidence? If you go back to the start of Part 2 and re-read it, it could free you up!). The nines are all about needing one last push, or one more person to help you over the line, asking for help and gratefully accepting it (even if it isn't up to standard). Nines are about being grateful for the other angels who come into your life; and about you, being the angel for others.

While the Lover was alone, she relished the chance to learn. She spent time with the High Priestess, listening to her wisdom and praying with her daily. It was a peaceful time. The High Priestess showed the Lover how to be her true self, no matter what was happening around her, and regardless of the influences of others. The Lover gained in maturity, knowing the one truth of all: be careful what you wish for.

Eventually, the Lover went on her way. She was strong in her gentleness, and confident in her hopefulness. This is how she came to be on the mountain, alone, the night her daughters were born under the soft light of the starry sky.

The morning after, the Empress appeared. She had been walking, showing her little ones the forest. She felt compelled toward the cave, and found the Lover with her babes. Newborn babes! Here was someone who needed the Empress's help. The Empress tended to the Lover and taught her how to be a mother, offering her a home and help in the years that came after.

Don't just draw those times, but draw the relief felt when that help was offered! The strength gained from reinforcements! We need to own our imperfections and realise that we all need help. Even I need proof-readers and editors! What? You thought all of these were my original words?!

TENS ARE TOO MUCH OF A GOOD THING!

You're there! You have reached the pinnacle! The mountaintop is yours! I want to tell you a great story that is from the night my mother breathed her last breath on this earth. While Mum was still sleeping, I took Dad, and one of my sisters, home from hospital for dinner and a nap. While at my parent's house, I had a bad dream that my elder sister rang to say, "come now" and I asked if it had happened or was about to. That sister said it hadn't happened yet. Still in my dream, I told my sleeping sister and Dad, and my father fell to the floor. The next scene in my dream showed my parents lying in two beds in the same hospital room: I didn't know who would go first. I was so moved by this dream that I got up and went looking for tissues. I found them, and my father came to me and wrapped his arms around me to comfort me. My sister at the hospital rang as Dad went to check on dinner, which was cooking on the stove. Now, in reality, my elder sister said to come, and confirmed that Mum had just passed. I told both my sleeping sister and Dad together, and he didn't collapse; we went back up to the hospital.

I stayed in Mum's hospital room with her after Dad and my siblings left, and helped the nurse to prepare my mother's body for the morgue, and then I escorted her there. That night when I went to bed, I wasn't sleeping but I had a beautiful experience: Mum showed me her arrival into Heaven. I saw all the "old crowd" of friends and family who had passed before her, with their arms outstretched to embrace her, as she made her grand entrance to the biggest party of her life. Everyone's eyes were filled with light. By the time Mum had passed, her central vision had deteriorated with macular degeneration, but now her sight was perfect: I could see through her eyes to experience all she experienced. Colours and light, smiles and embraces! My heart was filled with joy. I realised a while later that I could see her light reflecting in the eyes of all those loved ones come to greet her. Her celestial light.

I tell you this because I want you to know that if death comes, it's okay. I can't wait to be with my parents again. You could say that they were the loves of my life. As of 2019, nothing has yet come close.

The tens of the tarot don't need to be as dramatic, but they are about completion, attainment, perfect harmony, bliss. You walk into a room, and everyone there loves you. You lie on a beach and think, I need nothing else! You have the home, security, a great neighbourhood, friends and family who love you. You have the baby after the labour.

Now, I invite you to think of those times when you've achieved something for which you have strived. Feel how it felt then. If you can't think of anything in the past, imagine something in your future: something that means everything to you! Draw your images in your four quadrants, like you've done for every section of this chapter. The love you want. The educational attainment for which you are passionate. The vocation or job that sustains you even if nothing else comes close. The contribution you make to others, whether they be family, friends, colleagues, clubs, teams, charities, communities, the environment ... you get the picture; you know the drill. Make your images colourful and even three-dimensional. Embellish each with metallics if you can, and glitter! Make your images pop!

The important thing is the feeling. Feel how it feels. I can't put it into words, because they're your feelings, and your own words!

Chapter 7: The teenagers of the Minor Arcana

Prince and Princess / Page and Knight

The last tarots we'll talk about are the ones I like to think of as teenagers. In some decks, they are depicted by knights (adolescent and young adult males) and pages (adolescent and young adult females); in other decks they are depicted as princes and princesses (respectively). Do you remember what it was like to be that age? I do ..

When I was a teenager, I believed that nobody loved me, and I cried (a lot)! The older I got, the more I discovered that most teenagers were just like me. Not all were, just many (there is no way I'm going to minimise the onset of many mental health issues). The point is, we all get a bit "out of whack" during that period, up to the age of 35!! Alright, 25 .. The frontal lobes of our brains are still developing, and the changes between 12 and 25 can be really hard to cope with (for everyone). Confusion sets in, and we don't know if we can trust that the "vibes" we get are our intuition or imagination. We need to learn discernment.

We passionately launch ourselves into relationships, activities and tribes, with little (or no) thought of the consequences. We're indomitable. We're superheroes. And then, we're heartbroken, listless, lost, hopeless and helpless. Adolescence is a roller-coaster ride.

In the previous section, we talked about the aces to the tens – eleven cards that embody each stage of life as it turns around on the

[RE]BIRTH

wheel of fortune. Those cards keep happening throughout our life, because nothing changes if nothing changes, and let's face it: life is full of changes. The court cards embody our adolescent and adult selves; the graduation of who we are when we learn life's lessons. They're still in those four suits of love, communication, vocation and contribution (or Cups/Hearts, Swords, Wands, Pentacles), so we mature in each part of our life, sometimes at different stages. Take the teenager who gets their first job, or their driver's licence: this young person has independence! If they still live at home with their parents, they might rebel against the rules that have stood the test of time, because now they have a way out. They have power, just not all the power. The teenager who falls in love for the first time has a different power, because the power of love makes you confident you can do anything. You get the picture.

With each new job, course, significant other, we grow. When we get with a group that encourages charity or working to make our earth a better place, we also feel empowered and we mature because we are surrounded and supported by our elders who care.

The flipside to this, though, is when we don't have access to education (let alone continuing education), or transport, or money. When we run with the wrong crowd, things go awry, and it is very hard to get ourselves out of that whirlwind of darkness. Somehow, you need to get off the wrong tracks and save yourself; you need to find the people who will support you in being the best person you can be. There are many organisations that will help, both church-run and otherwise. And you never know, sometimes strangers will give you the hand-up that you need.

So here, I want to invite you to draw your last images: the times when you needed to grow up, and how you did it. The people who were there to either hold you back or lift you up. The resources required for that push over the edge of adolescence. The first love. The first course you chose to do. The first job. The first trip without your parents. Embellish with love, because these were the times that you needed more love than many others. Give yourself that love now.

Part 3:
Bringing it all together

Do you understand yourself a little better? I don't mind if you didn't do all the drawings; it is, afterall, your own book! But did you notice that when you took the time, that things came to you? Did you notice that when you coloured and defined and embellished, that you gave yourself and all the others in your life that little bit more love?

Did you find yourself being more forgiving? Did you feel more compassion? Are you a kinder person now? Are you more determined to make the world better by your phenomenal presence?

Now is your chance to think deeply about what you would like to do, what legacy you would like to leave the world.

Transform your relationships

It's time now to pull it all together and bring your newfound self into happy healthy relationships with others. You've learned to take some time to consider certain things about your life, yourself, and your behaviours. What you have learned about, are Antecedents, Behaviours, and Consequences (or ABC, for short).

An antecedent is something which leads to something else. It could be a "cause", as in Thing 1 caused Thing 2, but it might not be that simple. It could be a condition, an environment, a place, or a feeling, just as much as it could be a person (including yourself). The behaviour leads to something else. Let's imagine that you think a colleague is gossiping about you. The antecedent is your belief.

What are you going to do about it? Will you confront your colleague and force them to confess and apologise? Will you ask them about it gently, or attack them? Will you wait for evidence before saying anything? Will you stay silent every time they're near? Will you spend lots of energy avoiding them? All these options are behaviours, and they will all lead to consequences, even avoidance! The consequences are different for each behaviour. The point is, you have three things to consider before you decide what you will do: **ABC**. All three parts to the story are important, and you have control over what you believe and what you do, as well as some control over what you cause. Throughout this book, you have pondered these very concepts.

You have also pondered **feelings**. You've thought about your feelings and the feelings of others in the past. Now and into the future, think about how you would prefer to feel. It's likely you would prefer to be happy, healthy in mind and body, and that those you love will be happy too. You can always make this choice. There's a beautiful saying, "What would love do?". Choose love, over fear, every time.

We've thought about your life, and especially your childhood. You would probably agree, that **we need to protect children better**. Children have the right to grow up loving and respecting their parents, and that means their parents must be kind and protective of them. Parents and grandparents: please encourage everyone to speak nicely to children. Please don't swear or raise your voice; please don't hit or smack. Please know what abuse is, and stop yourself and others from perpetrating it. Please set rules that help your children learn respect for others and respect for themselves, as well as consequences for when they're naughty. They need rules and consistent consequences to reduce their feelings of anxiety. If you say, "do your homework" and they don't, you need a consequence, and you need to be consistent with it. If you say, "if you don't do your homework, you can't go outside to play" but you let them go outside anyway, you are not being consistent. They grow up thinking you don't mean what you say (which could eventually fester into "you can't be trusted", which could in turn become "the world can't be trusted").

Is this how you want your child to grow up? I don't think so. Children should be given tools to live their lives; and understanding rules, consequences and consistency will help them immensely. Try it for eight weeks. If it doesn't work, try something else. But, be consistent!

Transform your learning and teaching

You've been reminded in this book that it's good to keep on learning. Learn from others. Learn from Elders. Find mentors. Always keep looking for courses that will expand your mind, and experiences that help you to gain wisdom. One day, you will find the need to share your wisdom. I won't stop you. The fact is, you will certainly become an elder yourself: you will go through life's natural initiations, you will graduate to higher levels and become the master. Allow this to happen and welcome it, and remember to lead with compassion.

Transform your work and vocation

With continuing education, whether formal or informal, you will become sought-after. Be open to change when it does you good! Be open to transforming the work of others with gentleness and compassion. Lead always by your example. Be the shining soul you were made to be.

Transform your community

You don't need to be wealthy to do good for your community. You can help at a local community garden, hospital or nursing home – there are plenty of people who can't do everything for themselves. Elderly people in nursing homes often say how lonely they are because their family has placed them in care, but no-one ever comes to call. When

I was a massage therapist, I used to visit and wash their feet before giving them a foot and hand massage – the respectful touch and mutual attention were so good for all of us! You can help a charity to raise awareness or funds to do good work. If you do have more money than you need, then the #1 priority is reducing homelessness. Did you know that people who are homeless risk victimisation, bullying and physical abuse? They have trouble receiving government pensions if they have no home address, and those who live in accommodation provided by support services often fear for their personal safety (and the safety of their children). Many people who are "lucky enough" to couch-surf, risk being abused sexually and physically.

People who are homeless have higher risks of suffering depression, anxiety and trauma, as well as other more severe mental illnesses, and homelessness can exacerbate their symptoms. If you have money, please do what you can to help homeless people, even if it is giving someone your last note so they can buy a cup of coffee. Give a little dignity.

Transform the world!

So finally, I'm going to suggest a little Natural Hedonism. When we talk about mindfulness mediation, we talk about a calm presence: being aware (in an open, curious and non-judgemental way), being present (to oneself, the situation, and others), and being grateful. I like to take it one step further and just enjoy something in the moment. I appreciate the fact that I can breathe without difficulty, and walk without tiring too soon. I love that the sunshine feels warm on my skin and I'm able to protect myself from the sun's harshness, so I can enjoy the warmth a little bit longer. I love the rain falling on my garden. Little things that cost me nothing: I am not just grateful; I enjoy. While hedonism might not be that good for you, Natural Hedonism is!

So, now I invite you to enjoy the little things about your friendships, families, vocations, neighbourhoods and communities. Enjoy the small moments that bring you closer to God or perfection. Let little roses fall from heaven into your life and into your heart.

About the Author

Dr Mary-Claire Hanlon, Newcastle (Australia).

Dr Mary-Claire Hanlon was born the youngest of nine children and grew up in Newcastle, a coastal city just north of Sydney in Australia. Mary-Claire went to Sydney to seek her fortunes (or distractions, depending on your view) when she was aged 19, and returned to Newcastle to be nearer her parents when she was 30. Although no fortune found her, in the material sense, her life has been blessed with the other treasures – beloved family, dear friends, good health, great education, and the experiences of travel and vocation.

She completed her Bachelor of Science (Honours in Psychology) as a mature-age student, followed by a PhD (Psychiatry), and has attained various other academic achievements. She has over 15 years' experience providing clinically diagnostic, cognitive, intellectual and functional assessment of persons aged 16 years and over, and has conducted research since 2003.

Mary-Claire uses social-organisational psychological techniques to creatively produce cultural and individual changes, in her business, The Centre of Serendipity(https://www.TheCentreOfSerendipity.com). She facilitates workshops for small and large groups and individuals. Her workshop participants constantly agree that they love the unexpected things about her workshops. Participants always feel empowered by Mary-Claire's workshops. Mary-Claire's workshops are perfect for adults as well as young people, in all stages of life, and teams from every type of business. She is an engaging educator and speaker, awarded for international and national presentations on her mental health research. Additionally, Mary-Claire hosts RE[BIRTH] Workshops for small groups, in which participants enjoy Self-Transformation over Tea and Tarot.

FURTHER (MORE SCIENTIFIC) READING

Asato, M. R., Terwilliger, R., Woo, J., & Luna, B. (2010). White matter development in adolescence: A DTI study. *Cerebral Cortex, 20*(9), 2122-2131. doi:10.1093/cercor/bhp282

Brain Development Cooperative Group. (2012). Total and Regional Brain Volumes in a Population-Based Normative Sample from 4 to 18 Years: The NIH MRI Study of Normal Brain Development. *Cerebral Cortex, 22*(1), 1-12. doi:10.1093/cercor/bhr018

de Guibert, C., Maumet, C., Jannin, P., Ferré, J. C., Tréguier, C., Barillot, C., . . . Biraben, A. (2011). Abnormal functional lateralization and activity of language brain areas in typical specific language impairment (developmental dysphasia). *Brain, 134*(10), 3044-3058. doi:10.1093/brain/awr141

Decety, J., Michalska, K. J., & Kinzler, K. D. (2012). The Contribution of Emotion and Cognition to Moral Sensitivity: A Neurodevelopmental Study. *Cerebral Cortex, 22*(1), 209-220. doi:10.1093/cercor/bhr111

Frith, C. D. (1996). Brain mechanisms for 'having a Theory of Mind'. *Journal of Psychopharmacology, 10*(1), 9-15.

Gallagher, H. L., & Frith, C. D. (2003). Functional imaging of 'Theory of Mind'. *Trends in Cognitive Sciences, 7*(2), 77-83. doi:10.1016/s1364-6613(02)00025-6

Gallagher, H. L., Happe, F., Brunswick, N., Fletcher, P. C., Frith, U., & Frith, C. D. (2000). Reading the mind in cartoons and stories: An fMRI study of 'Theory of Mind' in verbal and nonverbal tasks. *Neuropsychologia, 38*(1), 11-21.

Hanlon, M. C., & Quidé, Y. (2018). Detecting an intention to communicate from non-word sounds. *Psychology and Neuroscience, 11*(2), 180-192. doi:http://dx.doi.org/10.1037/pne0000108

Holt-Lunstad, J., Smith, T. B., & Layton, J. B. (2010). Social relationships and mortality risk: a meta-analytic review. *PLoS Med, 7*(7), e1000316. doi:10.1371/journal.pmed.1000316

Isaacowitz, D. M., & Riediger, M. (2011). When age matters: Developmental perspectives on "cognition and emotion". *Cognition & Emotion, 25*(6), 957-967. doi:10.1080/02699931.2011.561575

Kitchener, B., & Jorm, A. F. (2002). *Mental health first aid manual.* Parkville, Australia: ORYGEN Research Centre.

Laurens, K. R., Luo, L., Matheson, S. L., Carr, V. J., Raudino, A., Harris, F., & Green, M. J. (2015). Common or distinct pathways to psychosis? A systematic review of evidence from prospective studies for developmental risk factors and antecedents of the schizophrenia spectrum disorders and affective psychoses. *BMC Psychiatry, 15*, 205. doi:10.1186/s12888-015-0562-2

Martin, G., & Pear, J. (1999). *Behavior modification: What it is and how to do it* (6th ed.). Upper Saddle River, New Jersey: Prentice Hall.

Minagawa-Kawai, Y., van der Lely, H., Ramus, F., Sato, Y., Mazuka, R., & Dupoux, E. (2011). Optical Brain Imaging Reveals General Auditory and Language-Specific Processing in Early Infant Development. *Cerebral Cortex, 21*(2), 254-261. doi:10.1093/cercor/bhq082

Mullinar, L. (2019). *Heal for life: How to heal yourself from the pain of childhood trauma*. Broadmeadow, Australia: Heal For Life Foundation.

Saxe, R. R. (2009). Theory of Mind (Neural Basis). In W. P. Banks (Ed.), *Encyclopedia of Consciousness* (pp. 401-409). Oxford: Academic Press.

Schurz, M., & Perner, J. (2015). An evaluation of neurocognitive models of theory of mind. *Frontiers in psychology, 6*, 1610. doi:10.3389/fpsyg.2015.01610

Senju, A., & Johnson, M. H. (2009). The eye contact effect: mechanisms and development. *Trends in Cognitive Sciences, 13*(3), 127-134. doi:10.1016/j.tics.2008.11.009

Uhlhaas, P. J., & Singer, W. (2011). The Development of Neural Synchrony and Large-Scale Cortical Networks During Adolescence: Relevance for the Pathophysiology of Schizophrenia and Neurodevelopmental Hypothesis. *Schizophr Bull, 37*(3), 514-523. doi:10.1093/schbul/sbr034

Wong, K. K., & Raine, A. (2018). Developmental Aspects of Schizotypy and Suspiciousness: a Review. *Curr Behav Neurosci Rep, 5*(1), 94-101. doi:10.1007/s40473-018-0144-y

www.ingramcontent.com/pod-product-compliance
Lightning Source LLC
Chambersburg PA
CBHW060341080526
44584CB00013B/866